Keys to High School Success

Get Your Homeschool High School Started Right

Lee Binz,
The HomeScholar

First Printing, 2015

Printed in the United States of America

ISBN: 150897571X
ISBN-13: 978-1508975717

Disclaimer: Parents assume full responsibility for the education of their children in accordance with state law. College requirements vary, so make sure to check with the colleges about specific requirements for homeschoolers. We offer no guarantees, written or implied, that the use of our products and services will result in college admissions or scholarship awards.

Keys to High School Success

Get Your Homeschool High School Started Right

What are Coffee Break Books?

Keys to High School Success is part of The HomeScholar's Coffee Break Book series.

Designed especially for parents who don't want to spend hours and hours reading a 400-page book on homeschooling high school, each book combines Lee's practical and friendly approach with detailed, but easy-to-digest information, perfect to read over a cup of coffee at your favorite coffee shop!

Never overwhelming, always accessible and manageable, each book in the series will give parents the tools they need to tackle the tasks of homeschooling high school, one warm sip at a time.

Everything about these Coffee Break Books is designed to suggest simplicity, ease and comfort - from the size (fits in a purse), to the font and paragraph length (easy on the eyes), to the price (the same as a Starbucks Venti Triple Caramel Macchiato). Unlike a fancy coffee drink, however, these books are guilt-free pleasures you will want to enjoy again and again!

Table of Contents

Chapter 1

The Love for Your Child Will Ensure Success

Sometimes I meet parents who are looking for THE specific key to homeschool success. Unfortunately, no-fail formulas don't work for everyone, but there is one foundational guideline my midwife gave me the day my eldest son was born, which comes close. She handed me my baby and gave me the only advice I needed, "Know your child and trust yourself."

When you homeschool, you will know your own child well and can trust your own instincts. Some people seem to think there's a magic wand they can wave to make everything work out, but it's the love you have for your child and knowing your child well that will ultimately make the difference.

One day while I was getting my hair done, I overheard two moms talking about their children in public school. One of the moms was describing how her child did not succeed in a Pre-Algebra class because it was too hard for him, but the public school insisted that he move on to Algebra 1. She didn't think it was a good idea, but the school wouldn't let him retake Pre-Algebra. They didn't want him to be left behind.

She asked her son how it was going during the first weeks of Algebra 1, and he said that he was lost, had no clue what was going on, and that he was going to fail. Two weeks into the quarter, she learned that the school had accidentally signed up her son for a Calculus class. Instead of taking and failing Algebra, he was taking and failing Calculus!

As homeschool parents, we're not perfect, but there's no way to make this mistake in our homeschools! We know our children and what they are capable of, so there's no way we'd skip through three levels of math and put them in a class way over their heads. In public schools, there is an average of 350 students assigned to every high school guidance counselor. Counselors don't usually know the student at all; when the student goes in for some advice, the counselor knows very little about them. Even if you are half as good as a high school guidance counselor, you will still be a hundred times more effective! It is the love for your child that's going to ensure your success; you care deeply about what is in their best interests, so you're not going to hurt them.

If we don't do a good job preparing our children, we might be financially responsible for those children for the rest of our lives! More importantly, we also have a huge emotional investment in their success, because we want them to do well. High school guidance counselors work to the best of their abilities, but they don't know each child. You don't need to feel hesitant about your own abilities, or feel that your child needs an official guidance counselor. You are what's needed; you're the best person for the job.

Advantages

Homeschooling high school has so many advantages for a student that sometimes it's hard to see why anyone would choose anything else! The first thing most people recognize is high academic performance. It's true; homeschoolers have higher academic achievement levels than their non-homeschooled peers, no matter the education level of the parent. Statistically, parents who do not have a high school diploma are almost as effective at educating their children as parents with a doctoral degree. In addition, homeschoolers have better academic preparation regardless of how much or how little the state intervenes. When you homeschool, your child can be fully educated, whether you use an outside educational program or put the curriculum together yourself.

Gender and race don't matter, either. Homeschoolers have better test scores than their public-schooled peers, regardless of the gender or race of the child. Even your income doesn't matter; you can produce a better-educated child as a homeschooler. Of course, that does not mean your child will always be in the 87th percentile. It means that by pursuing your child's best interest through homeschooling, they will be better educated than they would be in public school.

Homeschooling is the best learning environment for a child. It is safe and secure. You don't have to worry about their physical safety, their socialization, or negative feedback about their ability levels. Instead, they'll be stronger individuals, who will learn more without being distracted by other things. The socialization homeschoolers experience is the socialization of the whole world.

When you're homeschooling, your children have a lot of time to explore their interests. They are not locked onto a certain path based on whether they're mathematically or artistically inclined. Instead, through trial and error, they can explore a wide variety of different interests to find out what they'd like to pursue after they graduate. The time and space available through homeschooling gives students room to explore and experiment. That is what I call the homeschool advantage!

Chapter 2

Structure, Guidance and Survival

One of the keys to success in high school is to incorporate margin into your family's life. It's not just the vocabulary that makes some books easier to read than others; it's the amount of white space on the page! You want to have that space in your life, too. All the activities your child engages in may be wonderful, but you can't do it all. You will probably need to say "no" to a lot of good options in order to include some margin and keep your sanity. Having free time in your homeschool allows your kids to develop their God-given gifts and passion.

Provide Guidance

In addition to planning for margin, success in high school means being a good guidance counselor and advisor for your student. Many parents don't feel confident in this role. Think back to your own high school experience; did your high school advisor know you as a person among hundreds of school kids? Unless a child makes trouble or is an outstanding student, usually their public school advisor doesn't have the time to get to know them well.

As homeschool parents, we know our children intimately, more than any other person. You can feel confident advising your children, because you know them, and have the benefit of a 1:1 student/teacher ratio. If you think about what colleges want, you will feel less overwhelmed. Colleges simply want to see good academics, good test scores, and extracurricular activities. You can supply proof to colleges, just as a public school counselor can, but with the advantage of knowing your child better.

When you are your student's homeschool advisor, it's important not to drop the ball. Stay on top of things such as the academic calendar: when to study for tests, what year to take the tests, and what tests to take. My husband works as a project manager, but he doesn't build the buildings; he manages the people who build the buildings. That's your job as a homeschool advisor; you are the project manager when it comes to graduating from high school and applying to college. You don't write the essays, but you make sure your child completes and turns them in; you don't take the test, but you make sure your child takes it.

Encourage Leadership

If your child has thoughts of college, one of the skills colleges like to see is a demonstration of leadership. Sometimes when homeschoolers think of leadership, we only think of being student body president, but there are a million ways to demonstrate leadership skills.

Some kids can learn leadership skills through teaching a Sunday school class or becoming an Eagle Scout. Other kids, especially if they're quiet and reserved, can gain leadership skills through teaching another student a skill, such as playing guitar or piano. Colleges also like to see community service. As parents, we try to have our children involved in serving the community, and colleges like to see this, too.

Teach Survival Skills

Whether your high school graduate is heading off to college or simply moving out on their own, teaching survival skills is important. Before my children were seniors in college, I would have said the most important things to teach college-bound kids were note taking, public speaking, and essay writing. I asked my children, and they said, "Yes, those are important." Then I asked them what I should say to people to help them prepare their kids for college. They told me I should advise parents to teach students how to study. So, take advice from the experience of other college students and teach your high schooler how to study!

In order to be successful in college, teach your children the importance of sleep as well. I heard lectures about college students who didn't sleep, but I thought that would never happen to my children. Of course, it did. I think the solution is to have them write an essay every year about the importance of sleep. They still may not sleep when they go to college, but you won't have to nag them about it, because they will already know their brain won't function and their body will fall apart if they don't sleep. Try to teach them this in high school!

Chapter 3

Choosing High School Curriculum

A successful high school experience owes much to selecting the right curriculum for your kids. One of the most important keys to choosing that curriculum is to invest in your weaknesses. Put your curriculum budget money in your weakest area first. When you identify a weakness, whether it's math, foreign language, or art, for example, make sure you invest your money to supplement your weakness.

Your weakness is also where you're most willing to make mistakes. If you fail with your math curriculum, perhaps your child hates it and has a fit every single day, then invest in this weak area and try something else. Your strengths will handle themselves. If your strength is art, you're going to do art naturally.

Weaknesses are also where you should put your time first. If your children have a weak subject area, that's the first thing they should work on each day. As soon as they get it done, they can move on to things that aren't so difficult. Working on weak areas is also what you should still try to do when things fall apart in your life. If everything else must go by the wayside, try to get the work done in your child's weak area. (It's helpful to implement consequences if a student doesn't complete their work in their weak area - grounding is effective for teenagers.)

Another aspect of investing in your weaknesses is investing in your own education as a homeschool parent. When I was a nurse, continuing education was required every year. Homeschool parents need to educate themselves as well. Ask yourself these questions. Do you know how to homeschool at the next level? Are you comfortable with tenth or eleventh grade, if that's next? That does not mean you have to pre-read every book your student will use, or that you have learned calculus before your child does; it just means you are learning how to homeschool high school.

You don't need to be the one who teaches everything to your child. There is going to come a time when you turn to a video tutorial for the first time. Just because you use a video tutorial does not mean that you have failed as a homeschool parent. On the contrary, once you've taught your child how to self-teach, you've met your goal. Your goal in life is to hand them something and have them learn it all on their own. That's what they have to do when they get to college, and when they get a job. The first time you turn to a video tutorial, and the first time you can't teach the subject and they're learning it on their own, you'll know that you're successful.

Do What Works

The next key to choosing high school curriculum is to continue doing what works. If what you have been doing through elementary and junior high is working, keep doing it. If the curriculum is working, keep using it. The same techniques will always work, whether you're teaching high school or younger students.

At the high school level, make sure that you are using a curriculum made for homeschoolers. If you're teaching a subject you don't know, buy a curriculum meant for homeschoolers, because a curriculum meant for a classroom assumes the teacher is already an expert.

Learning to homeschool high school is much like letting your child learn how to ride a bike. You want to keep that forward momentum towards developmental milestones, so you don't fall down. Keep going forward, even if that means you have to do a Calculus class next year.

Allow Input

Allowing your teen to have input is one of the most important keys to choosing curriculum. This becomes even more important as they get older, because when kids grow up, they're starting to become adults. It's not just about their learning style or your teaching style anymore; suddenly personal preference comes into play.

Sometimes your child won't like watching their video tutorial anymore because the teacher uses a white board instead of a black board. Maybe they don't like that the person teaching on a particular video has a Southern accent, because it drives them batty. If you ask why they don't like something, they may not be able to verbalize why; they just have personal preferences, the way that adults have personal preferences.

One of the most important areas you can let your child give input in is math. Almost everyone will rely on a video tutorial for math at some point, and it's not going to be you learning calculus, it's going to be your child. Make sure it's a good match.

At Their Level

The last key is to teach your student at their level, in every subject, all the time. One of the reasons public schools and classroom settings have such a hard time educating kids is that students are in classes based only on their age. Just because a child is 14 or 15 doesn't mean they should take American history, algebra, or specific topics in English. Make sure your child is able to work at their own level.

Chapter 4

Recommended Courses

One of my foundational beliefs about homeschooling is that parents know the best way to educate their children. A parent's knowledge about their student's learning style can help in selecting courses they should take in high school. If your child is planning to attend college after high school, or you even think they might consider it, it's important to plan their high school curriculum with that in mind.

Regardless of what your state might require for high school graduation, think about college admission requirements and set your goals according to them. In Washington State where I live, we get to decide on the graduation requirements for our children. I know a homeschool dad who required both of his daughters to take a calculus class in order to graduate. Likewise, if you set college preparation requirements as your own graduation requirements, your student will be prepared for college, whether they plan to go now or later.

Here is a list of recommended courses to take in high school, courses that colleges look for in their applicants. As you read it, think about how you can incorporate these subjects into your homeschool.

English

If you ask most colleges, they'll tell you they like to see four years of English, but there's a variety of ways you can meet this requirement. Your student could study literature and composition through a prepared curriculum, or you could simply have them do reading and writing every year. You might want to consider a speech class as an alternative. One year, one son wanted to take third year Latin but the other wanted to do first year French. One wanted to do *Sonlight Language Arts* but the other wanted to use *Learn to Write the Novel Way.* I wanted to please everyone so we ended up doing EVERYTHING! I do NOT recommend this strategy! (Unless, of course, you enjoyed the pain of childbirth.)

Math

It's important to have four years of math on the transcript. It's less important what LEVEL of math they do each year. Colleges like to see kids moving forward in their math studies, so just teach your student consistently at their level. It's great to complete Geometry before the PSAT test in eleventh grade, and better still if your child can complete Algebra 2 and Pre-Calculus before taking the SAT test. As long as you do the next thing, working on math at their level, you can't lose.

Social Studies

Most colleges also require social studies, and like to see three to four years of this core course. Usually this will mean world history, American history, American government, and economics courses. Our favorite supplement in this area was *The Great Courses*. These are college level lectures on audio or video. My kids loved them! You don't have to choose the expected classes for social studies, either. One year, one of our sons took a Russian History course and the other chose Psychology. Remember, not every subject has to involve tests. Sometimes you can just audit a course as they do in college. That is how we used *The Great Courses* lectures.

Science

Include three years of science for college preparation, with at least one lab science. We covered biology, chemistry, and physics classes, each with a lab component. Each area of science is so different that a child may hate one but love another, so it's helpful to try to expose them to each area. You can also branch out into different subjects, such as geology or astronomy. Colleges love to see unique courses!

Foreign Language

Many colleges require a foreign language for admission, so be prepared. The best advice I ever got about foreign language is to do a little every day. A daily 15-minute study period is a much more effective way to study than once a week for an hour. We used foreign language curriculum designed for homeschoolers (who don't already know the language). Remember, you don't always have to know a subject to teach it. You only have to know where to find a good curriculum (a homeschool convention is a good place to start), and then let the student learn independently.

Physical Education

Some kids find it EASY to get the required two credits of PE. They get PE credits through playing on a soccer team, summer swim league, or community running clubs. Some kids, however, hate physical exercise! Other ways to obtain physical education credits include becoming involved in a yoga class, or weight lifting at the local YMCA. Your children could also take CPR or a health course at a community center. Some kids who hate PE will love going swing dancing, or downhill skiing. Any physical activity that breaks a sweat counts!

Fine Arts

Colleges like to see some fine arts on the transcript. Not being an artistic family, we had to look up fine arts in the dictionary. I learned that fine arts include music, art, theater, and dance. Who knew? There are many opportunities to find those credits. Some choose to take music or art lessons, but there are other, more budget-conscious ways to get credits. My kids didn't like hands-on projects, so we studied the fine arts through history using library books. We also studied music history by checking out CDs and biographical books on different composers and styles of music.

Electives

Some of the most valuable electives to include are driver's education, typing, logic, and computer skills. These are skills adults need every day. They either have them or wish they did. Make sure your student has the time to pursue their passion, too. A little known secret is that their passion IS an elective! I had a student that loved chess and studied it for hours each week. One year in high school, we called those credit hours "Critical Thinking." The next year, when he began teaching chess classes, we called it "Public Speaking." The following year he had multiple chess-related jobs, and we called the course "Occupational Education." I know students that have specialized in ornithology (birds), fungus, economics, and musicology. Time for specialization is one of the benefits of homeschooling, so seize this opportunity!

How Can You Do It?

So how do two normal parents with only a tenuous grasp of algebra and a casual relationship with grammar, teach children upper math and Latin? The answer, my friend, is to "cheat" by using people who are much smarter than you to help you through the rough spots. For example, there are MANY great video tutorials for every level in math – some of them even demonstrate the solution to every problem in the book. Where do you find these resources? At a homeschool convention or curriculum fair, where you can compare different choices side-by-side. Don't forget to bring your kids. Sometimes, the best thing to do for the hard-to-please teen is to give them ownership of the curriculum choice. Our oldest son shocked us all by choosing Saxon Math for high school calculus. Mom and Dad, who grew up thinking a math book had to have pretty pictures to be effective, were dismayed. However, it seemed to work for him. Kids today!

Chapter 5

Struggling Learners

No matter what your child's age, dealing with learning challenges can be difficult. In high school, it can become seriously concerning. You don't have to be afraid! With the great student-to-teacher ratio in your homeschool and the love you have for your child, you have what it takes!

One of my friends was at her lowest point when she realized her twelve-year-old son could not read or write in his Sunday school classes. She had to shield him carefully from the judgment of others. Her homeschool friends were very understanding, but she worked hard to keep him away from situations where he would have to read aloud. She was distraught. Again and again they changed curriculum, hoping each time that a new one would change everything. It seemed like nothing would ever work. He struggled with learning all the way through high school. She never had him officially tested, because she didn't want him to carry that label as an adult. He has achieved wonderful things since graduating homeschool!

When he turned 18, he started working at Starbucks. An excellent worker, he received nothing but positive feedback, which motivated him to continue his education. He decided to attend college. He didn't score well on the SAT, so they did not report his scores to colleges. He entered college through the back door, by attending community college first. His excellent work ethic and love of learning helped him thrive where others felt adrift. Dan transferred from community college to the university with a 3.89 grade point average. There were 300 applicants to the business school that year, and Dan was one of only 100 admitted. His mother said, "He finally realized he could do it!"

This mom has some great advice for parents. Don't push them before they are ready. She was glad she kept him home, so that he could avoid the negative feedback from a public school setting. She read aloud to her son constantly – even his high school textbooks, when necessary. She used verbal assessments in all his classes, and didn't introduce essay writing until much later.

She recommends books by Dr. Raymond Moore, including *Better Late than Early: A New Approach to Your Child's Education* and Grace Llewellyn's book, *The Teenage Liberation Handbook: How to Quit School and Get a Real Life and Education*. She also recommends Cynthia Tobias' book, *The Way They Learn*. She says, "You feel like you're failing – like you didn't do something right." Don't be deterred, though. It takes a lot of one-on-one time, but that's the benefit of homeschooling. Read textbooks aloud to them, along with the classics.

In her lowest moments, she remembered her grandfather. He also could not read. His wife would read him blueprints each night to prepare him for work the next day. Her grandfather was still a successful businessman. He was able to compensate, just as her son is able to compensate now.

Her biggest surprise was realizing that her son wanted a college degree. She had never thought he would go to college, and only vaguely considered a technical school. But when he worked at Starbucks, he identified his gift in business. Her additional advice is the same as mine. She says, "Even if you think they won't go to college, they may – so always be prepared!"

Her son is so thankful he was homeschooled. He says he would never put his own children in public school. He knows that if he had been in public school, he wouldn't be where he is today. Nurturing is critical, and homeschooling can provide the best. This mom ends with some encouragement, "I remember the hopelessness. They CAN succeed and excel – just give them the tools."

Learning to Teach

Another friend, JoAnn, homeschooled her two daughters, feeling extremely unsure of her own abilities until her girls were officially diagnosed with learning disabilities. Once she had the diagnosis, she realized that homeschooling was the best option. She didn't want her girls ostracized and placed in a "special" group that would have a negative effect on their socialization skills. Even JoAnn's mother became increasingly supportive of homeschooling after the diagnosis.

Her two girls could not read until halfway through fifth grade. They struggled in reading, writing, and spelling. JoAnn took her children to *The Slingerland Institute for Literacy*. She recommends two pamphlets that helped her cope: "Why Wait for a Criterion of Failure" and "An Adaptation of the Orton-Gillingham Approach for Classroom Teaching of Reading" both by Beth Slingerland.

JoAnn's advice is, "Never despair! The timing of brain growth is on your CHILD'S timetable, not yours. Accept it, because you certainly can't change it!" She wishes she had dropped more academic subjects when they were in elementary school. Still, she is so glad she homeschooled. "Homeschooling is better for dyslexic kids for the positive encouragement and socialization."

She taught with multi-sensory input and multi-sensory output. In every subject, she worked to provide lessons with audio, visual, AND tactile input. She supplemented courses with drama, hands-on projects, and verbal assessments all the way through school. Her daughters found the use of color especially helpful. Her daughter still color-codes her college lecture notes to improve her level of retention.

JoAnn's older daughter went directly into a university and majored in biology with a minor in chemistry. She graduated with an advanced degree as a veterinarian technician. JoAnn's younger daughter also went directly into a university, and graduated with a degree in interior design; she even did some design work for

Bill Gates as a college intern! Both girls were very successful in college.

Learning to Cope

Sue was hesitant about labeling her daughter in any way, but knew she faced some unique challenges even though she didn't have a formal diagnosis. Her daughter became a National Merit Scholarship Semi-Finalist. Here is what Sue said about her daughter's struggles:

> "She worked hard and I'm very proud of her. She is the daughter that would fit into the statement, 'I could never homeschool my child because ...' She is very active, intense, dramatic and a joy to be around. I am convinced that if she were in the public school, we would have been 'encouraged' to put her on medications (the standard line around here when she is getting jumpy is to, 'Run up to the mailbox and get the mail,' which is a mile round trip). She has forced me to think outside of the box, and it is an

adventure I'm sorry to see come to a close."

Like other mothers I've mentioned, Sue was able to find a way to harness strengths and weaknesses, and teach her child to compensate for difficulties. With a parent's close attention, unique coping mechanisms can develop. A homeschooling parent can see small successes, and learn to shape and mold to find new ways of coping with each challenge.

Joelle is right in the thick of things, with her young child. I asked her for some advice for others, and she emphasizes that coping comes from faith. This is Joelle's experienced advice:

> "A learning 'disability' (a word I hesitate to use for anyone who doesn't have a severe condition) isn't something you can just make go away if you have a clinic and a handful of web links. A learning challenge is best addressed with being sensitive to learning styles

and interests, which, as you know, vary from child to child.

A learning challenge is also a mindset, a lifestyle, and sore knees from prayer. A learning challenge means you'll come face to face with your pessimism and lack of faith through tears of mourning for the child you don't have. But lest anyone abandon hope, a learning challenge also means seeing God answer those tears by turning them to tears of what is, hands down, absolutely the most incredible joy when you see the triumphs. You will see those victories sooner or later on Earth or in Heaven.

A learning challenge leads to personal growth in the siblings of the challenged child. A learning challenge is a worldview, a lens, a perspective. It's the fierce mother-bear love you have when you whisper to your child, 'Don't listen to the naysayers. I love you no matter what, and I'm still your teacher.'

I can't put this in a box. I can offer a short list of resources, but there's only one resource here that I can guarantee hands down will help everyone. The rest can be labeled 'of interest.'

1) *The Bible.* Children are people – in fact, they are the most human of people. There are many passages on how we are to deal with our fellow humans. This is the only resource on this list that I can guarantee WILL help.

2) *Last Child in the Woods: Saving Our Children From Nature-Deficit Disorder* by Richard Louv – read this concurrently with *Smart Moves*, below

3) *Smart Moves: Why Learning Is Not All in Your Head* by Carla Hannaford – which will probably lead to curiosity about *Brain Gym*, below

4) *Brain Gym* or similar therapies offered by the two associations, below

5) *The National Association for Child Development*

6) *The Developmental Movement Center*, Seattle (206) 525-8038"

Learning to Grow

Jay Smith of Linfield College says this:

> "The advice that I'd give to your students is to simply be proactive in their college search process. The students shouldn't be afraid to ask colleges if they offer support for students with learning disabilities, and what that support entails. We have high expectations of our students, but we also understand that we all learn in different ways."

Some colleges have a supportive environment for children with learning disabilities. Redeemer Pacific College is a small Catholic college in Langley, BC, affiliated with Canada's premier Christian liberal arts university, Trinity Western University. Admissions Coordinator Jennifer Friesen says, "All RPC students are able to use the services for students with disabilities offered through TWU, including access to the Learning Resource Centre and starting off their university career at TWU's Freshman Academy." The Learning Resource Centre offers services such as note taking, accommodated examinations, and provides material in alternate formats.

At Redeemer, Freshman Academy is a program for students who have not met the requirements for admission into university due to a low grade point average or missing academic courses. Friesen says, "Freshman Academy allows students to go through their classes in a small cohort with the support of their professors, a faculty Learning Coach, and their classmates. Once students have completed Freshman Academy they are able to directly enter their second year of university at Redeemer Pacific and Trinity Western."

When I go to college fairs, I notice how many colleges truly specialize in students with learning struggles. They WANT your students, and they are ready, willing, and able to teach them.

Learning to Succeed

You can request accommodation for the SAT and ACT if necessary, which does require a doctor's diagnosis. If you don't want accommodation for the college admission tests, a diagnosis may not be necessary. You may feel comfortable with your homeschooling methods, and don't feel the need for additional help or direction. Perhaps a specialist will not affect what you're doing, and a diagnosis may not change anything or be worth your while. On the other hand, if you are completely baffled about how to teach your student in a way that makes sense, and the input of a specialist will help you and change what you are doing, then evaluation may be useful.

If you think a diagnosis will help YOU, then I think it will help your child. In that situation, testing would be worthwhile, even if it's inconvenient. If testing will not help you, then it may not be necessary.

Keep in mind your long-terms goals. You want your child to grow up and have his own home. You want your child to succeed and thrive in anything they choose. Some colleges specialize in learning disabilities. There IS a great college out there for your child, and they will understand and accept any learning issues without hesitation. Search and you will find just the right college.

Chapter 6

Finding the Fun Factor

You know your children are going to goof off. At some point, you'll be wishing they were doing something productive, instead of just having fun.

But wait! Isn't that what homeschooling is all about? One of the big benefits of homeschooling is having fun while learning at the same time! Having FUN during school hours can be a meaningful and significant way to learn important (although sometimes elective) subjects.

When kids are homeschooling and having fun, that's awesome! Here are some ideas for how to translate that fun factor, and maximize their transcript and career plans!

Identify the Fun

When writing a homeschool transcript, start with the easy subjects. Begin with subjects that use curriculum, or require your attention: English, math, social studies, science, foreign language, PE, and fine art. Once you get to the end of that list, many parents feel stumped. Now what? Ask yourself the first big question.

What do they do for Fun?

When I'm helping parents with a transcript, that one question can open the floodgates! How does your child spend unstructured time? When they are supposed to be working on schoolwork or emptying the dishwasher, what are they doing instead? That can be a great indication of their Fun Factor.

If they enjoy their fun for more than one hour a day, you may be able to translate it into a high school credit. Anything involving music, band, handcrafts, or theater can be a fine art credit. You can award an occupational education credit to children who love starting their own business or working with a small business, from yard work to online marketing. Children who love creating or fixing computer hardware or software can get credit for computer technology. If children love something that makes them sweat, give them credit toward PE, whether it's dance, a gym membership, team sports, or individual athletics. Kids who love speech and debate may earn a credit each year. Some children will love a specific TOPIC, such as mushrooms, birds, or horses. Others will love a specific IDEA, such as economics or politics.

Maximize the Fun

Public schools offer fun classes, too. The only problem is that their fun classes are primarily fun for the teacher. In high school, I took a class called Polynesian History because my teacher liked to travel to Hawaii every year. It was fun, but it wasn't my thing. It was my teacher's interest. It's a lucky student who loves the same elective as their teacher.

In a homeschool, the equation is different. The student can decide what fun classes to take instead of the teacher. That's great news! It means you don't have to like it yourself and you don't have to teach it yourself. Your job is to scoop up those high school credits so they don't get lost. Your mission is to find value and a future in the areas your child loves.

How it's Done

Estimate how many hours they spend on their Fun Factor. Is it one hour or more each day for most of the school year? That is enough for a 1-credit class. I think it's helpful to keep their love to just one credit per school year. If their Fun Factor has two distinct skills, and they spend many hours per day, then it can make sense to count it as two classes.

If you are stuck on a class title, do a little research. Do they take a class or lessons from an expert? What is that class called? If you need more help, try to find a college that offers a class in the subject. What is that class title? For example, when you search for "horse community college" you can find classes called Horsemanship, Equine Fitting and Grooming, Equine Facilities Maintenance and Mechanics, Equine Anatomy and Physiology. Look at the descriptions for each class to find the one most similar to what your child does. It can provide both the name of your class and the beginnings of a course description.

For some students, their favorite pastime may make them famous. A singer may envision becoming the next American Idol. A golfer may be determined to make it to the Masters. A computer geek may imagine himself the next Steve Jobs or Bill Gates (depending on if he is a Mac or PC person, of course)! These pastimes turned into careers have one thing in common, money and huge amounts of it. Sure, it may not be likely, but you can still use the possibility of a lucrative career when guiding your child. Instead of denigrating their potential, take it out for a test drive. Talk to your child about what they will do if they strike it rich with their Fun Factor.

What if they Strike it Rich?

They will need to manage their money and their business, market their skills, and avoid being taken advantage of or swindled. All of these things are related to one college degree: business. A business degree is a common degree at most 2-year and 4-year colleges. They require a variety of classes, but not an excessive amount of math or science. Regardless of their interests, a business degree can help them manage the day-to-day process of turning a profit, while giving them the knowledge they need to advance their career.

What if they don't Strike it Rich?

A business degree is also useful for something else, though. If something happens, and they don't become famous, or they change their mind or become unable to complete their dreams, a business degree is a great safety net. Many entrepreneurs and corporations search for business generalists – the students who can adapt to almost any job description. In the meantime, beginning college as a business major can be an excellent springboard for other degrees.

Not every career requires a college degree. In the battle between college and dropping out to form a band, there is a middle ground: business school. If you want your child to go to college, and they want to focus only on what they love, I can suggest a conversation like this ...

> "I see your talents in this area, and it's possible you might become famous. I want you to be prepared. Many famous people are cheated or swindled, and I want to make sure that doesn't happen to you. Consider getting a degree in business. You will learn how to handle your money, read a contract, and make money with your skills. Get more information about it. Go to a college fair, and tell them what you are interested in doing. Ask if they offer scholarships. Colleges may give you scholarship money, paying you to go to college and practice your skills. Instead of paying for a teacher or mentor,

waiting years for the chance to play, you'll be performing or competing right away. And then after college, you'll be able to use the degree to further your career."

In my Gold Care Club conversations and transcript consultations, I spend lots of time helping parents find the Fun Factor. I begin with a simple question, "What does your child do for fun?" That question alone can usually generate options in the electives category. No curriculum is required; we just work together to scoop up learning for fun. When that question doesn't bring a huge response, then often a second simple question is required, "What does your child do that drives you crazy and what annoying thing do they do instead of schoolwork?" If the "fun" question doesn't work, the "annoying" question is usually fail-safe.

Don't Be Embarrassed

I was helping one mother with her transcript, and she hesitated when we got to the "fun" question. I could tell she felt embarrassed about something. Finally, she blurted it out, "MMA – he loves mixed martial arts. He is training and taking lessons and has already completed a class in boxing."

Showing embarrassment is so common among parents. We just don't understand how our kids can love something that we don't love. After all, God has called us to do something, and it's easy to assume that means our children have the same calling, but that's not necessarily the case. Secondly, it's easy to feel that our child has fun in a bizarre and abnormal way. While that may sometimes be true, it's usually not. Third, many parents worry that I'll be judgmental. I'm not. I've had boys. I've homeschooled teenagers. I understand there are some things you can control and other things you can't!

That's when I had to confess my understanding of MMA. You see, my husband is a fan. While I'm reading *The Help* or a Jane Austen book, my husband watches mixed martial arts. Sure, I'm not happy about it. As a nurse, I can't believe that people are intentionally trying to cause brain damage. As a wife, and as a mother of boys, I can understand how that happens. I know that GSP has a *fleur de lis* tattooed on his right calf, that Brock Lesner used to wrestle in the WWE, and that Chuck Liddell is not famous because of *Dancing with the Stars*. I may not enjoy it myself, but I can understand it. That's so true for many other things as well. Don't be embarrassed. It's OK.

My mission is to help all parents homeschool high school. I don't judge your homeschool or evaluate your children. I come alongside, as a friend, willing to help in the context of your situation.

Chapter 7

Academic Records

One of the most important aspects of homeschooling high school is to keep good records. You'll need these records when it comes time to apply for college, scholarships, work, internships, and any number of other situations.

How to Forget Four Years of Latin

A while ago, I was working on a transcript for a high school junior. I met with the mom and student, and we went over every subject area in detail, from high school algebra to American Sign Language. Everything was complete. As I was leaving, I asked, "What are you doing this weekend?" Mom didn't hesitate for a moment, but explained that they were going to a Latin competition that weekend.

"Latin?" I said. "You never mentioned Latin!" That was how I discovered that her high school junior had already completed four years of high school Latin, and her mother had completely forgotten about it.

It's not like the four years of Latin was a repressed memory of something horribly traumatic. It was obvious that the student enjoyed it – that's why she was still competing. This points out why you want to keep high school records. It's not just so you don't forget that your child did a two-week unit study on economics. It's so you don't forget broad swaths of learning, such as four years of Latin.

Keep high school records so that when the time comes, you can make a transcript that reflects the courses you taught. Keep records so that you don't short-change your student. This mother is a gifted home educator, and has done an exceptional job homeschooling her children, and even SHE forgot four years of Latin. Never underestimate the human ability to forget! It can happen to anyone!

Four Kinds of Homeschoolers

When it comes to record keeping, I have noticed that there are four kinds of homeschoolers. There are people who keep records in big plastic tubs, who I call "Tubbies." They keep all their records from all of their children in that tub, and it's a perfectly acceptable method of record keeping.

There are parents who keep records in cupboards, cabinets or drawers. Slightly more organized than Tubbies, "Cubbies" will usually have one drawer for each child and for each year. This is also a fine method of record keeping, and it has the added benefit of organizing information by year.

Still other parents keep a notebook with their high school records, and it's also a useful method of keeping records. I am one of these "Binder Queens" myself. I will go into depth about this method in the next section.

The final type of homeschool parents are the ones I affectionately refer to as "Question Marks." When this type of parent hears about record keeping, a question mark will appear over their ever-so-slightly-cocked head as they think to themselves, "Records? Were we supposed to keep records?" I do NOT recommend this method! That's how you can lose things like four years of Latin, or the years your child spent as an Eagle Scout.

Homeschool parents can decide which method is best for them. Tubbies keep lots of stuff but lack organization. Cubbies keep many records with minimal organization. Binder Queens have information on every class in an organized fashion. I usually recommend that parents try to get more organized each year. If the first year you are a Tubby, try to graduate to a Cubby the next year. Move up the food chain!

The Binder Method of Record Keeping

When we first started visiting colleges, I asked the admissions staff what records they wanted me to bring. They said, "Bring them all!" I was astonished, but I did what they wanted. I traipsed into the admission office with six binders full of homeschool records – one binder for each year of high school for each child. By the look on their faces, I quickly determined that perhaps they weren't interested in necessarily SEEING my records; they just wanted to know that I HAD records. Using a binder system was convenient for me, because it was a convenient place to keep something from every class. If they ever wanted to see something from Latin or Macroeconomics class, all I had to do was reach into a binder for a work sample.

What do you put IN the binder? My binders were 3-inch, 3-ring binders, each with a creative title such as, "Kevin Senior Year." Inside the binder, I had about twenty, labeled dividers. In the front, I had records I needed to keep for colleges and to meet our state homeschool law. The first section was for the transcript, which I made once they finished each year. Then there were sections for the Declaration of Intent to Homeschool, immunization records, and annual testing records, because our state law requires them. I had a section for their reading list and a list of my kids' activities and awards.

Finally, I had a section divider for each class that I intended to do that year: math, English, history, science, etc. In the beginning of the year, that was all it said: "math." Later in the year, usually in the spring, I would go back over what we had taught and develop a course description for each class. I noticed that by having a PLACE for records, I would KEEP records. Like my bank records, they weren't often filed like they were supposed to, but once every couple of months, I would methodically take all the papers they produced and gradually fill in that three ring binder. I was able to see easily which sections were filling up, and which sections were blank.

What to Keep

How do you know what records to keep? For some classes it's relatively simple, just keep any tests or papers they have written, and you're done! For other classes, you may want to keep their lab reports, research papers, or work sheets.

Some classes don't have paper assignments; then what do you do? Last spring, a mother was talking to me about record keeping, and she asked what records she should keep for her child who was learning how to cook at home. The answer is, BE CREATIVE! Think methodically about what they DO for the class. In the cooking example, the mother mentioned that her daughter created a menu, did the shopping, and cooked using recipes. Why not use this information for records? Save the menu and shopping list, and photocopy the recipes she uses – those are your records for your culinary arts class. My sons play piano, and I had a similar dilemma. We didn't have any reports or homework for piano, so we kept a list of songs they learned to play, the piano books they used, and we saved the programs from their recitals.

There are other ways to keep records. Keep a reading list of every book they buy, use, or read for pleasure. Keep track of how many hours you spend on subjects that aren't "bookish." The credit value of courses such as PE, fine arts, and electives may be hard to quantify unless you keep track of hours. You can keep course descriptions from co-op classes. Some people will photocopy the cover and table of contents from textbooks.

These methods will help if you want to make a course description for your classes. If you write assignments for your kids or have a schedule for them, keep them. You can also do it the opposite way, and instead of writing down what you want them to do in the future, you can write down what they DID do. That will help parents who are conscientious, but not into planning. You can also have the student keep a journal of all their schoolwork. That would never have worked for my kids, but I know it works for others. Make sure they include every book, assignment and experience. Most students will do some of their work on the computer. You can save all of it in a file, or print it, or both.

When to Keep Records

Homeschool records become critical once students begin high school and they become part of a transcript colleges will see. How do you know when your child is in high school? In general, public school children are considered high school age at about fourteen-years-old, or once they reach ninth grade. One of the delightful "problems" with homeschooling is that it isn't always easy to label your child's particular grade level. I started keeping records in seventh grade, so that I would train myself to keep records and be competent by the time they were in high school. When my youngest son was fourteen years old, he took and passed some CLEP exams (which measure college level learning). This was a strong clue for us that he was probably already beyond high school in many subjects! Because I'd been keeping records to "train myself," we were able to collect enough information to make his transcript when we needed it. If your child is in seventh or eighth grade, consider being prepared and keeping your homeschool records as if they were already in high school. As you are training yourself to keep records, strive to keep SOMETHING to document every subject they learn. Keep records often! It's a rare person who will update records every day, but everyone can put record keeping on their calendar every month or two.

Right now, why don't you decide whether you will be a Tubby, Cubby or Binder Queen (or King) this year?! Get prepared now, and then throughout your school year spend some concentrated time collecting records for your homeschooled high schooler.

Chapter 8

The College Preparation Process

College preparation is a process, not a moment, and where you should be in that process depends on the age of your child. In addition to staying with the process, I always encourage parents to be looking ahead to the next thing down the road, so they're ready when it comes!

Middle School

If you have a middle school student, your goal is to either review or preview. Middle school is the time to do remedial work with your student if they don't quite know their basic math facts. It's also a time for previewing high school. If your child is ready to learn algebra or geometry in seventh and eighth grade, that is a perfectly fine time to teach those classes to your middle school student.

For parents, this time is about practicing homeschooling high school. If this was high school, what would you write for course descriptions, how would you make transcripts, and what classes would you teach? What you don't want to do is wait until ninth grade and panic!

When children take a preview class or do something that's at a high school level, you can put that on their high school transcript. I've seen classes that kids took in seventh and eighth grade on public high school transcripts. If your child does high school level work, you can put it on their transcript regardless of their year.

Freshman Year

Freshman year is when you start to think about and prepare for college. Plan ahead, learn how to homeschool high school, and start the transcript. By working on your transcript every year starting in ninth grade, you won't forget any courses by the time your child graduates.

Sophomore Year

Sophomore year is when you start to plan for college. First, have your child take the PSAT. Although not every child takes the PSAT, it can be helpful. While it does not count towards scholarships as a sophomore, it is good practice for when your child takes it as a junior and it does count. The PSAT is only available in October every year, so you have to sign up in September.

By sophomore year, your student should have started a foreign language. If you haven't started in freshman year, start in sophomore year so that you can potentially get three years done if your child likes it. Even if you took two years to finish a one-year curriculum, you can still make sure two years are done by the time they graduate.

Junior Year

The first task for junior year is to take the PSAT; the PSAT taken in junior year is the one that qualifies your child for the National Merit Scholarship. It's the one that counts for big money.

Your second task in junior year is to find colleges your child wants to attend. Attend a college fair, so you can learn about the wide variety of possibilities. There are many college fairs all over the country, just make sure to find one and go.

You also need to visit colleges. It's important that you visit colleges, because you won't know what they're like unless you see them. If it's important that your child attend a Christian college, you won't know whether it's a Christian college in practice (or is just Christian in name) unless you go visit.

The next task for junior year is to make sure your child takes the SAT or the ACT. Take the test that makes your child look like a genius.

By the end of junior year, you want your child to have decided on a handful of colleges where they want to apply. They will apply in senior year, so you should have some choices ready by the end of junior year.

Senior Year

In senior year, your goal is to have those college applications in before Christmas, because scholarship money is given out on a first-come, first-served basis. The sooner you get your application in, the better chance you will have of getting the scholarship money, and the easier it will be to get housing.

If your student tested poorly as a junior, you can have them repeat the SAT or the ACT test in senior year. If they didn't take it during junior year, you can still take it in senior year. Lastly, remember to make plans for a great high school graduation party!

Conclusion

Assurance from Scripture

I want to conclude by reminding you of one of the most important keys to high school success, which is to not be afraid. God assures us in Scripture that we don't need to be afraid. The love for your child is going to ensure success. Let's look at a few specific Scriptures for assurance.

Psalm 139:13-16 says:

> "For you created my inmost being; you knit me together in my mother's womb. I praise you because I am fearfully and wonderfully made; your works are wonderful, I know that. My frame was not hidden from you when I was made in the

secret place, when I was woven together in the depths of the earth. Your eyes saw my unformed body; all the days ordained for me were written in your book before one of them came to be."

These are the verses usually discussed in terms of the abortion debate. They remind you that your child was given to you and your family, whether you gave birth to that child or not, that child is yours, and was placed into your family. You are the perfect person to parent them, and you have what it takes.

The second scripture is Philippians 4:13, which says, "I can do all things through Christ who gives me strength." It doesn't say that you are capable of all things except homeschool, and it doesn't say that you're capable of all things except calculus. It says that you can do all things.

The last scripture is 1 Peter 4:8, which says, "Above all, love each other deeply, because love covers a multitude of sins." Even though our children have been given to us, and even though we're capable of everything, we still are sinful people who make mistakes. However, when you know that the love for your child is going to cover any missteps that occur, you release yourself from having to be a perfect homeschool parent. That's not going to happen, so just be the loving parent that you are. When missteps occur in your homeschool, love will cover a multitude of sins.

Appendix 1

Suddenly Single: Single Parent Homeschooling

Death, divorce, and deployment can happen, leaving even a homeschool parent suddenly single. It may happen suddenly, and unexpectedly. When you are a single parent, it's important to remember that you are NOT alone!

Mary Jo Tate of *Single Parents At Home* explained what happened to her.

> "I never expected to be a single mother. When my husband left me, I was shocked, angry, and scared. I was embarrassed to be divorced; for a while I felt as though I wore a scarlet D emblazoned on my dress.

Our four sons were bewildered, and their world was turned upside down. I was deeply committed to remaining at home with my children and continuing to homeschool them, yet I wondered how I could support us all financially."

When a parent becomes suddenly single, homeschooling may seem an even more daunting task. Now what? How can you continue in the challenging lifestyle you love? The trick is to adapt, and find a new normal for your family. Find resources and achieve a balance that works for you.

Find Income and Emotional Support

The problem is two-fold. As Mary Jo explains:

"In many homeschooling families, the dad takes primary responsibility for earning the living and the mom takes primary responsibility for educating the children. The labor is divided and the support is multiplied. Although there are also many two-parent families where both parents contribute to the education and the finances — often through a family business — a single parent is often solely responsible for both. The labor is multiplied and the support is subtracted."

The single parent must find the solution to two problems: financial income and emotional support.

When I was homeschooling, our group had two suddenly single parents who joined forces. Sally and Kate each continued to homeschool and both had to work to support their single parent households. They each had two children. They decided to share the load. Sally worked as an office assistant three days a week, while her friend homeschooled the four children. Kate worked as a dental assistant three days a week while Sally homeschooled the four children. Together they functioned as a co-op. Each one would create assignments for their own children, but their friend would supervise when they had to go to work. It was a great arrangement that was unique and worked for them. Each family will find a path that will work in their own situation.

If you have been homeschooling, you can continue to homeschool your children. If you are single, you can begin homeschooling your children. Whether faced with death, divorce, or deployment, there are resources available to assist you.

Deal with Pressure

Alice, a homeschooling single parent in Virginia, was eager to share her experience so others could be encouraged.

> "Single moms get pressure from every side. That is for sure. Single parents have many challenges, and compassionate, no-nonsense help is what we need. People will put pressure on a single parent in all sorts of ways. They will pick at many different areas, and a homeschooling single parent has to know and believe in their heart that they are doing what God has directed them to do. I have many

years under my belt as a single parent, and there were many times when I would cry over my budget, and feel so alone, wondering how I was going to raise my children. God never left me. We never went hungry, and I always paid my mortgage on time. Having a support system helps, but it takes time to build that too. Talk to people and ask for help."

She had to find a way that worked for her family. She found that she had to change her strategies over time.

"Praying and seeking God is the first thing to do. I do whatever I need to do to survive financially. I have had jobs where I have taken my son when he was small. Right now, I clean houses. I have tried working part-time and full-time jobs and that works too, if you can find a flexible schedule. Trading with other single moms/dads can work. Even bartering services can fill in areas. I have done so many different things at different times. God has always provided for my children and myself. Part of the key is to keep faith and listen only to sources that edify and enforce what God says. Guard your heart and your mind from naysayers, even the ones that mean well."

Resources for the Single Homeschool Parent

For a list of clickable resources to help you face homeschooling with confidence, including websites, articles, and videos, see:

www.TheHomeScholar.com/suddenly-single.php

It's important to remember that God's promises have not changed, even if your situation has changed. Watch my Scripturally based YouTube video called "How you know you can homeschool high school?"

Minimize Change

Aside from the homeschool issues, I can suggest one other thing, limit the amount of change as much as you can. Something dramatic has happened in your children's lives. Try to prevent any other change from happening if you can. Keep their school the same, their home the same, and their schedule the same, as much as possible. Experts suggest limiting the stresses you can control, especially during the first year. You may not have control over some things. Obviously something will have to change, but if housing and child support are provided, then perhaps some of the other changes can wait. Visit your church (or a large church in your area) and ask to speak to the pastor for advice and resources.

Finally, if you have a friend who is a single parent, particularly if they are homeschooling, there are specific ways you can help. Mary Jo says:

> "If you are a single parent, don't be afraid or too proud to ask for the help you need. Others are blessed

by ministering to you. If you want to help single parents, however, don't wait for them to ask. Volunteer your assistance, or ask what they need."

Appendix 2

Coffee is the Key to Homeschool Happiness!

That might be overstating it a bit, but not by much. It doesn't have to be coffee, of course, any refreshment will do. But I do LOVE a nice cup of coffee!

1. Coffee can help you have your morning meeting with your kids

When you meet with your children each day and go over your expectations for them, the whole day will go more smoothly. A quick daily check-in is often all it takes. It reminds me a lot of having a quiet time. In fact ...

2. Coffee can help you have your morning meeting with God

When you meet with the Lord each day and He goes over His expectations for you, then your whole day will go more smoothly. A quick daily check-in with the Bible can be just the encouragement you need to stay on course.

3. Coffee can encourage you to take care of yourself

If you engage in some self-care, you'll be much more capable of other-care. We do so much for others all day long that a bit of me-time can start the day off right. It doesn't have to be coffee, it can be tea or a warm meal, but taking care of yourself is the first step toward taking care of others. Remember what the airlines say, "First, put on your own oxygen mask."

4. Coffee can encourage budding friendships

Having coffee with another homeschool

mom while the kids play can increase the chances of adult friendship, too. Instead of dropping them off, stay and enjoy fellowship with others. We crave the company of someone other than our children and sharing a coffee can encourage sharing our feelings.

5. Coffee can encourage understanding of others

The best support system I had was my weekly cup of coffee with my best friend. She shared her struggles with learning disabilities and I shared my woes about my own children. We both ended up with a better appreciation for the struggles others face.

6. Coffee can ensure you have margin

Everyone needs time in the day when nothing is planned. The margin of your day is like the margin in a book. Book margins make a book readable, and life margins make life livable. If you don't have time to sit down and have a cup of coffee, then you don't have enough margin in your life. Take a moment. Sip. Breathe. It's cheap therapy.

7. Coffee makes wonderful memories

Coffee can make a lasting, warm memory of friendship. I remember going to Starbucks once a week, while my son Kevin taught chess. It was just Alex and me in the coffee shop; he was studying and I was sipping my peppermint mocha learning about homeschooling high school. This created good memories to last a lifetime.

Afterword

Who is Lee Binz, and What Can She Do for Me?

Number one best-selling homeschool author, Lee Binz is The HomeScholar. Her mission is "helping parents homeschool high school." Lee and her husband Matt homeschooled their two boys, Kevin and Alex, from elementary through high school.

Upon graduation, both boys received four-year, full tuition scholarships from their first choice university. This enables Lee to pursue her dream job - helping parents homeschool their children through high school.

On The HomeScholar website, you will find great products for creating homeschool transcripts and comprehensive records to help you amaze and impress colleges.

Find out why Andrew Pudewa, Director of the Institute for Excellence in Writing says, "Lee Binz knows how to navigate this often confusing and frustrating labyrinth better than anyone."

You can find Lee online at:

www.TheHomeScholar.com

If this book has been helpful, could you please take a minute to write us a quick review on Amazon?

Thank you!

Testimonials

Grateful for the Gold Care Club

"Dear Lee,

Thank you, thank you, thank you!! My homeschool career is almost over. All three daughters are in university and the youngest is also in her last year of high school. They are doing so well, and much of that is because you walked me through those years when I thought, "Am I messing up my kids?

If only I could begin again – I'd be much more relaxed, I'm sure, and I would have been a Gold Care Club member throughout **all** the high school years!! I had never thought of many of the things you presented in your webcasts, ebooks, etc. The phone calls were also extremely helpful. Thanks again for the high school help.

All three girls will graduate from college together. I couldn't have done it without your help! They worked on much of their degree(s) before they even hit the University! I never would have thought they could do that without your insight."

~ Allyson

"Erased my fears"

"Lee,

I just want you to know that I regularly share your website with other homeschool moms who are homeschooling high school or will begin soon. You have been such a help and blessing to our homeschool journey through high school that I always highly recommend you.

Being my kids' high school counselor is probably the scariest position I have held as a homeschool mom, but you have helped me to be informed and to erase my fears. You are an incredible resource!

Thank you and God Bless You!!"

~ Kathy

For more information about my **Gold Care Club**, go to:

www.TheHomeScholar.com/ gold-care.php

Also From The HomeScholar...

- The HomeScholar Guide to College Admission and Scholarships: Homeschool Secrets to Getting Ready, Getting In and Getting Paid (Book and Kindle Book)
- Setting the Records Straight - How to Craft Homeschool Transcripts and Course Descriptions for College Admission and Scholarships (Book and Kindle Book)
- Total Transcript Solution (Online Training, Tools and Templates)
- Comprehensive Record Solution (Online Training, Tools and Templates)
- Gold Care Club (Comprehensive Online Support and Training)

- Preparing to Homeschool High School (DVD)
- Finding a College (DVD)
- The Easy Truth About Homeschool Transcripts (Kindle Book)
- Parent Training A la Carte (Online Training)
- Homeschool "Convention at Home" Kit (Book, DVDs and Audios)

The HomeScholar "Coffee Break Books" Released or Coming Soon on Kindle and Paperback:

- Delight Directed Learning: Guiding Your Homeschooler Toward Passionate Learning
- Creating Transcripts for Your Unique Child: Help Your Homeschool Graduate Stand Out from the Crowd
- Beyond Academics: Preparation for College and for Life
- Planning High School Courses: Charting the Course Toward High School Graduation
- Graduate Your Homeschooler in Style: Make Your Homeschool Graduation Memorable

- Keys to High School Success: Get Your Homeschool High School Started Right!
- Getting the Most Out of Your Homeschool This Summer: Learning just for the Fun of it!
- Finding a College: A Homeschooler's Guide to Finding a Perfect Fit
- College Scholarships for High School Credit: Learn and Earn With This Two-for-One Strategy!
- College Admission Policies Demystified: Understanding Homeschool Requirements for Getting In
- A Higher Calling: Homeschooling High School for Harried Husbands (by Matt Binz, Mr. HomeScholar)
- Gifted Education Strategies for Every Child: Homeschool Secrets for Success
- College Application Essays: A Primer for Parents
- Creating Homeschool Balance: Find Harmony Between Type A and Type Zzz...
- Homeschooling the Holidays: Sanity Saving Strategies and Gift Giving Ideas
- Your Goals this Year: A Year by Year Guide to Homeschooling High School
- Making the Grades: A Grouch-Free Guide to Homeschool Grading

- High School Testing: Knowledge That Saves Money
- Getting the BIG Scholarships: Learn Expert Secrets for Winning College Cash!
- Easy English for Simple Homeschooling: How to Teach, Assess and Document High School English
- Scheduling - The Secret to Homeschool Sanity: Plan You Way Back to Mental Health
- Junior Year is the Key to High School Success: How to Unlock the Gate to Graduation and Beyond
- Upper Echelon Education: How to Gain Admission to Elite Universities
- How to Homeschool College: Save Time, Reduce Stress and Eliminate Debt
- Homeschool Curriculum that's Effective and Fun: Avoid the Crummy Curriculum Hall of Shame!
- Comprehensive Homeschool Records: Put Your Best Foot Forward to Win College Admission and Scholarships
- Options After High School: Steps to Success for College or Career
- How to Homeschool 9th and 10th Grade: Simple Steps for Starting Strong!

- Senior Year Step-by-Step: Simple Instructions for Busy Homeschool Parents
- High School Math the Easy Way: Simple Strategies for Homeschool Parents In Over Their Heads

Would you like to be notified when we offer the next *Coffee Break Books* FREE during our Kindle promotion days? Leave your name and email below and we will send you a reminder.

http://www.TheHomeScholar.com/ freekindlebook.php

Visit my Amazon Author Page!

amazon.com/author/leebinz